WOMEN in STEM

By Rebecca Phillips-Bartlett

Minneapolis, Minnesota

Credits

All images are courtesy of Shutterstock.com, unless otherwise specified. With thanks to Getty Images, Thinkstock Photo, and iStockphoto. Cover – Amma Shams, balabolka, natsa. Throughout – Amma Shams. 4–5 – Gorodenkoff. 6–7 – Credited to 'Mr. Grey' in Crispin Tickell's book 'Mary Anning of Lyme Regis' (1996), Public domain, via Wikimedia Commons, Morphart Creation, NotionPic, AlyonaZhitnaya, Kariakin Aleksandr, GoodStudio, PavloArt Studio. 8–9 – Alfred Edward Chalon, Public domain, via Wikimedia Commons, Charles Babbage, CC BY-SA 2.0 <https://creativecommons.org/licenses/by-sa/2.0>, via Wikimedia Commons, topform, pantid123, kichikimi, balabolka. 10–11 – Everett Collection, Eve Curie: Madame Curie. S. 329 [1], Public domain, via Wikimedia Commons, nadiia__oborska, balabolka. 12–13 – Employee(s) of MGM, Public domain, via Wikimedia Commons, Abrarova Zukhra, Piyanat nethaisong, VETOCHKA. 14–15 – Njames0343, CC BY-SA 4.0 <https://creativecommons.org/licenses/by-sa/4.0>, via Wikimedia Commons, ValterDesign, GoodStudio, Ilya Oktyabr, Alexander__P. 16–17 – NASA, Public domain, via Wikimedia Commons, Wawx, Bonezboyz, NASA/Sean Smith, Public domain, via Wikimedia Commons. 18–19 – Bengt Nyman, CC BY-SA 4.0 <https://creativecommons.org/licenses/by-sa/4.0>, via Wikimedia Commons, Xinhua News agency, Public domain, via Wikimedia Commons, Maryna Gorbatko, Orfeev, korzuen, fire__fly. 20–21 – Tinseltown, Nick Greaves, farikha rosyida, Anna Sukhova. 22–23 – USFWS - Pacific Region, Public domain, via Wikimedia Commons, USFWS - Pacific Region, Public domain, via Wikimedia Commons, Anna Frajtova, Fagreia. 24–25 – Nadia Snopek, NASA-Starchild, Public domain, via Wikimedia Commons, GoodStudio. 26–27 – DASwartz, CC BY-SA 4.0 <https://creativecommons.org/licenses/by-sa/4.0>, via Wikimedia Commons, D-VISIONS, moloko__vector. 28–29 – Bühler, Mannheim, Public domain, via Wikimedia Commons, United States Geological Survey, Public domain, via Wikimedia Commons, U.S. Department of Labor, Public domain, via Wikimedia Commons, US Air Force, Public domain, via Wikimedia Commons, frozenbunn, Akevi. 30 – Sofia Gegel.

Bearport Publishing Company Product Development Team

President: Jen Jenson; Director of Product Development: Spencer Brinker; Managing Editor: Allison Juda; Associate Editor: Naomi Reich; Associate Editor: Tiana Tran; Art Director: Colin O'Dea; Designer: Kim Jones; Designer: Kayla Eggert; Product Development Assistant: Owen Hamlin

Library of Congress Cataloging-in-Publication Data is available at www.loc.gov or upon request from the publisher.

ISBN: 979-8-88916-978-9 (hardcover)
ISBN: 979-8-89232-514-1 (paperback)
ISBN: 979-8-89232-166-2 (ebook)

© 2025 BookLife Publishing
This edition is published by arrangement with BookLife Publishing.

North American adaptations © 2025 Bearport Publishing Company. All rights reserved. No part of this publication may be reproduced in whole or in part, stored in any retrieval system, or transmitted in any form or by any means, electronic, mechanical, photocopying, recording, or otherwise, without written permission from the publisher. Bearport Publishing is a division of Chrysalis Education Group.

For more information, write to Bearport Publishing, 5357 Penn Avenue South, Minneapolis, MN 55419.

Contents

She Who Dares 4
Mary Anning 6
Ada Lovelace 8
Marie Curie 10
Hedy Lamarr 12
Mamie Phipps Clark 14
Katherine Johnson 16
Tu Youyou 18
Jane Goodall 20
Sylvia Earle 22
Valentina Tereshkova 24
Sau Lan Wu 26

More Daring Women 28
Changing the World 30
Glossary 31
Index 32
Read More 32
Learn More Online 32

She Who Dares

People are always finding new ways to understand the world around them. Some people create incredible inventions to help make life better. We often turn to STEM—science, **technology**, engineering, and math—to help make these new discoveries.

> Think of a challenge you have in your daily life. Could you invent something to make things any easier?

From fossils to computers, our world is full of fantastic discoveries and inventions. Many advancements have been made by some very smart women in STEM.

SISTERS IN STEM

Throughout history, women have had to overcome extra challenges to be recognized for their outstanding achievements in STEM. In the past, many schools did not allow women to get an education. Other schools let them study only a few subjects.

Many daring women have broken through all kinds of **barriers** to be able to work in STEM. They used their strength and intelligence to create new and exciting things.

Breaking through barriers takes lots of bravery and courage.

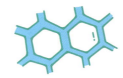

How do you find strength to overcome the challenges in your life?

Mary Anning

FANTASTIC FOSSIL FINDER

Born: 1799   **Died:** 1847

Mary Anning was born in the small town of Lyme Regis on the coast of England. As a child, she spent her days exploring beaches and searching for fossils with her father. At her church's Sunday school, Anning learned to read and write. Soon, she was teaching herself all about animals and rocks.

Anning's family was very poor. They often sold the fossils they found to help make money.

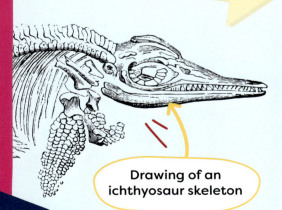

Drawing of an ichthyosaur skeleton

When Anning was 12 years old, her brother found a strange fossilized skull. Anning searched for the rest of the animal and carefully dug it out. She and her brother became the first people to find an ichthyosaur skeleton. This creature lived in the ocean about 200 million years ago.

Anning went on to discover many more incredible fossils, including the first pterosaur found outside of Germany. She was even the first person to suggest that a stone called coprolite was actually fossilized poop! Anning's discoveries have been used to learn about Earth's history. She is remembered as one of the most successful fossil hunters of all time.

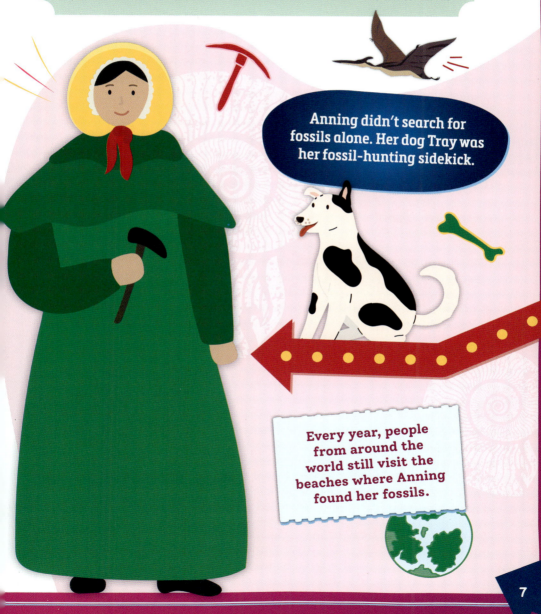

Anning didn't search for fossils alone. Her dog Tray was her fossil-hunting sidekick.

Every year, people from around the world still visit the beaches where Anning found her fossils.

Ada Lovelace

CHAMPION OF COMPUTING

Born: 1815 **Died:** 1852

Ada Lovelace was born in London, England. She learned French, Italian, and music. At the time, most women did not study math and science, but Lovelace did. She also experimented with machines.

> Charles Babbage's invention was called the Analytical Engine.

When Lovelace was 17, she met Charles Babbage. He was working on an invention similar to a calculator. Lovelace was fascinated by his project and began to work with him. She used her language skills to translate notes from another engineer about Charles' project. She even added many of her own ideas to the notes. Lovelace noticed that the invention used patterns and knew that it could do more than just calculate numbers.

Unfortunately, Babbage did not have enough money to finish the project and Lovelace's notes were forgotten. More than 100 years later, however, the notes were found and printed in a book about computer patterns. Even though she wrote long before the first computer existed, she had discovered how computers would work. Lovelace is often called the first computer programmer.

Today, there is a computer language named after Lovelace!

Marie Curie

X-RAY EXPERT

Born: 1867 **Died:** 1934

Marie Curie was born in Warsaw, Poland. The college in her town did not accept women as students, so she moved to France to study. There, she met her husband, Pierre Curie. Together, they made some incredible discoveries.

The Curies found two new elements called radium and polonium. Marie Curie studied these elements and realized that they could help save lives. The elements were radioactive, which means they give off energy that can pass through solid materials. Curie used this knowledge to help make **X-ray machines** that could take clearer pictures of the inside of the body.

During World War I (1914–1918), Curie invented moveable X-ray machines that fit in the back of trucks. They were called Little Curies. Doctors used them to help injured soldiers. Curie even drove one of the trucks herself!

In 1903, Marie and Pierre won a Nobel Prize in **physics**. This showed the world just how important their discoveries were. Marie Curie was the first woman ever to win a Nobel Prize. Then, in 1911, she won one in **chemistry**. She is the only person to have won a Nobel Prize in two different areas of science. Today, her discoveries are still used to help treat illnesses, such as cancer.

Radium is so radioactive that it gives off a faint bluish glow.

Hedy Lamarr

WONDER OF WI-FI

Born: Around 1914   **Died:** 2000

Hedy Lamarr was born in Vienna, Austria. Growing up, she spent her free time taking machines apart and rebuilding them to learn how they worked. She also loved to act. When Lamarr was about 17, she starred in her first movie. A few years later, she starred in another and soon became famous.

In 1937, Lamarr moved to Hollywood in Los Angeles, California, to continue her acting career. However, the world of science still interested her. She worked on creating inventions while acting in movies. After reading about fast fish and birds, she came up with designs for wings that allowed airplanes to fly faster.

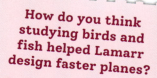

How do you think studying birds and fish helped Lamarr design faster planes?

During World War II (1939–1945), Lamarr wanted to help with the war effort. She invented a device that could send messages over a long distance.

Lamarr never made any money for her invention. However, her device helped people create other communication technologies, including Wi-Fi and cellphones. Lots of the tech we have today would not have been possible without Lamarr's work.

Lamarr is often called the Mother of Wi-Fi.

Mamie Phipps Clark

PSYCHOLOGIST AGAINST SEGREGATION

Born: 1917   **Died:** 1983

Mamie Phipps Clark was born in Hot Springs, Arkansas. At the time, many schools were **segregated**. This meant that Black and White children were separated and often treated differently. Because of this, Clark was always very aware of her identity as a Black girl.

College was expensive, but Clark was very smart and was awarded a **scholarship**. At first, she studied math. Later, she realized that she could help more people if she studied **psychology**.

Clark wanted to use her education to help children.

During her studies, Clark did an experiment with dolls to find out when Black children learn about race. She proved that segregation caused Black children to feel bad about themselves. Her experiment showed that it is better for all children when they learn and play together.

In 1954, Clark's work was used as evidence in court. Soon, it was ruled that segregated schools would no longer be allowed.

Katherine Johnson

MOON LANDING MATHEMATICIAN

Born: 1918   **Died:** 2020

Katherine Johnson was born in White Sulphur Springs, West Virginia. She always loved solving math problems. In 1953, she started working for NASA. Along with many other women, Johnson worked on the difficult math problems needed to send people into space.

But Johnson did more than just solve the problems. She asked lots of questions of her own. She even asked for an invitation to some very important meetings that women had not been allowed to attend before.

When Johnson started working for NASA, there was a lot of segregation. She broke through many of these barriers. By 1958, NASA was no longer segregated.

Johnson worked on many incredible projects at NASA. She calculated the path needed to send the first American astronaut into space. One astronaut trusted Johnson's math abilities more than that of a computer! He asked her to double check the numbers before he was launched into space. In 1969, she calculated the route for the first moon landing. Johnson's hard work and bravery changed the history of space travel.

Tu Youyou

MASTER OF ANCIENT MEDICINE

Born: 1930

Tu Youyou was born in Ningbo, China. When she was 16, she suffered from a disease called tuberculosis and had to take time off from school. This inspired her to study medicine so that she could stop other people from getting sick.

Tu set to work researching malaria, a disease that is spread by mosquitoes. To better understand it, she bravely visited places where people were suffering from **outbreaks**. But many other people were trying to find a cure, so Tu decided to do something different.

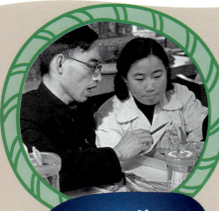

Tu studied how plants could be used as medicine.

Tu read ancient Chinese medical books to see how people thousands of years ago used plants to treat **symptoms** of malaria. After studying hundreds of plants, she discovered that one called sweet wormwood could be used to cure malaria. Tu and her team created a new medicine that has saved the lives of millions of people.

Tu Youyou was the first Chinese woman to win a Nobel Prize!

Tu was so confident in her medicine that she tested it on herself before giving it to patients.

Jane Goodall

WILDLIFE WHIZ

Born: 1934

Jane Goodall was born in London, England. As a child, she was very interested in animals and their behavior. She spent lots of her time watching, sketching, and making notes about animals. She dreamed of working with wildlife.

When Goodall was 26, she was given an incredible opportunity to go to Tanzania and study chimpanzees. She didn't have any scientific training, so she came up with her own methods of studying the animals.

Growing up, Goodall enjoyed stories that had lots of wildlife. They inspired her to learn about animals. How can your favorite stories inspire you?

Goodall studied chimps in ways that nobody had tried before. Some scientists criticized her and said that she was not scientific enough. But Goodall didn't let this stop her. She spent lots of time living with the animals to learn about their lives.

Goodall uses her work to encourage people to be kind to animals and the planet.

Unlike other scientists, Goodall gave the chimps she studied names instead of numbers. She noticed that the animals had **unique** personalities, social rules, and the ability to make tools. Goodall even learned how to communicate with the chimpanzees using sounds, body language, and facial expressions.

Goodall's favorite chimpanzee was named David Greybeard.

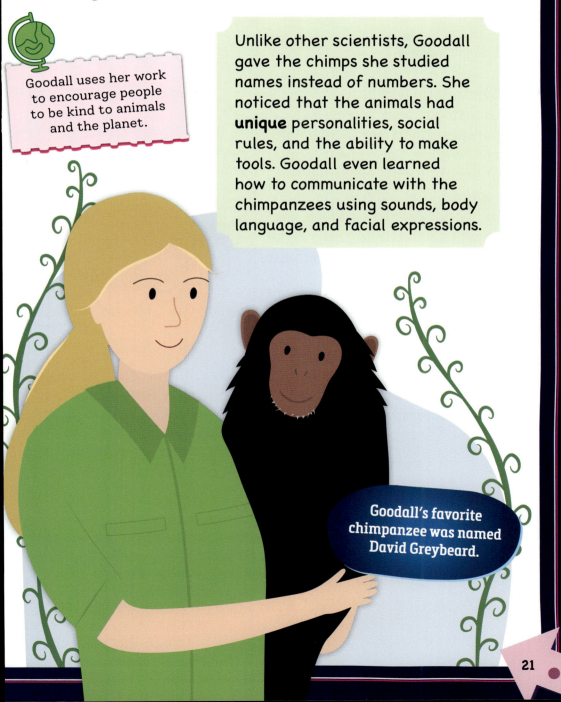

Sylvia Earle

DEEP SEA DIVER

Born: 1935

Sylvia Earle was born in Gibbstown, New Jersey. Her parents taught her to love nature and wildlife. Earle spent lots of her childhood watching the tadpoles that lived in the pond in her backyard. At college, she spent years studying how **algae** was important to ocean **habitats**.

Earle has gone on many diving trips in the ocean. She was the first woman to go 100 feet (30 m) below the surface in a **submersible**.

Soon, Earle became one of the most experienced divers in the world. She led an all-female team that lived 50 ft. (15 m) underwater for 2 weeks. She and her team studied the effects of pollution on coral reefs.

Earle broke the record for the deepest walk on the sea floor. She spent more than 2 hours walking about 1,250 ft. (380 m) below the surface!

Earle uses her underwater discoveries to teach people the importance of looking after the oceans and the wildlife that lives there. She was even named Hero for the Planet by *Time* magazine.

Valentina Tereshkova

FIRST FEMALE IN SPACE

Born: 1937

Valentina Tereshkova was born in Maslennikovo, Russia. She loved being in the sky. Her favorite hobbies included **parachuting** and skydiving.

When Tereshkova was 25 years old, she was accepted into Russia's **cosmonaut** training program. Unlike most in the program, Tereshkova had never trained as a pilot. However, her experience parachuting earned her a place in the course.

After more than a year of training, Tereshkova rocketed into space. She was there for almost 3 days and flew around Earth 48 times. She had become the first woman and the youngest person to go to space!

After returning to Earth, Tereshkova traveled to different countries to encourage other women to follow their interests in space. She has worked in politics and won many awards, including the United Nations Gold Medal of Peace.

When Tereshkova was in space, her radio call name was Chaika, which is the Russian word for seagull.

A crater on the moon is named after Tereshkova.

Sau Lan Wu

FANTASTIC PHYSICIST

Born: Early 1940s

Sau Lan Wu was born in Hong Kong. Growing up, her family was very poor, so she didn't go to a very good school. At first, Wu wanted to be an artist. Then, she read a book about Marie Curie's life and was inspired to study physics.

Wu moved to the United States to go to college. She applied to many schools but was not accepted because they didn't have scholarships or dorms for women. Finally, she was accepted to Vassar College in New York.

> Wu's dream to get an education gave her the courage to apply to college. How might your ambitions help you do something new?

Wu set a goal to make at least three big scientific discoveries in her life. She has already achieved this! She helped discover three different kinds of **particles.** Wu's discoveries have helped scientists better understand the universe and what it is made of.

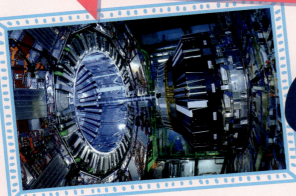

Wu uses a machine called the Large Hadron Collider.

More Daring Women

BERTHA BENZ and Her Courageous Commute

Born: 1849   **Died:** 1944

Bertha Benz was married to an inventor named Karl. He created modern cars, but many people didn't think the invention would be useful. In 1888, Bertha Benz became the first person to drive a long distance in a car. During her journey, she repaired the car using pieces of her clothes.

Benz's journey lasted more than 13 hours.

KATIA KRAFFT and Her Fearless Films

Born: 1942   **Died:** 1991

Katia Krafft and her husband made many films that taught people about the dangers of volcanoes. Often, they stood only a few steps away from burning lava while making the documentaries. Thanks to their brave exploration, we know more about volcanoes.

EUGENIE CLARK and Her Significant Swim

Born: 1922   **Died:** 2015

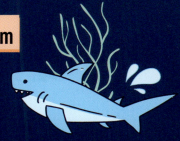

Clark was often called the Shark Lady.

As a child, Eugenie Clark spent a lot of time at the New York Aquarium. She was fascinated by the incredible animals she saw. As an adult, she swam with sharks in the ocean to study their behavior up close. Clark taught people about sharks to help them not be afraid of these wonderful sea creatures.

GLADYS WEST and Her Marvelous Math

Born: 1930

Gladys West grew up on a farm. But she always knew she didn't want to work on one. Instead, West wanted to be a mathematician. As an adult, she used math to create a model of Earth. West's model is used for **GPS** systems today!

Changing the World

Many women have worked hard to make new discoveries about the world. Whether they were inventing life-saving medicine, teaching others to protect the planet, or sending people into space, the world would not be the same without women in STEM!

The path to success was not always easy. However, these women had the bravery and determination to break through difficult barriers. They dared to be different so they could change the world.

Many people in STEM started out as curious kids. What are you interested in learning? How can you help make new discoveries?

DO YOU DARE TO CHANGE THE WORLD?

 # Glossary

algae tiny plantlike living things that grow in water

barriers obstacles that block or limit access to something

chemistry the science that studies the basic elements and how they function

cosmonaut a Russian astronaut

GPS Global Positioning System; a system that uses satellites to give location information

habitats natural environments in which plants or animals live

outbreaks instances in which diseases rapidly spread among groups of people

parachuting jumping out of a plane or helicopter using a soft cloth attached to ropes to slow down the fall

particles tiny pieces that things are made of

physics the science that studies energy and matter

psychology the study of the mind, emotions, and human behavior

scholarship an award that helps pay for someone to go to college

segregated forced separation of people, often by race

submersible a special vehicle designed for deep-sea exploration

symptoms signs of a sickness

technology the use of science to invent helpful tools or devices

unique special and unlike anything else

X-ray machines devices used to take pictures of the inside of someone's body

INDEX

animals 6, 20–21, 29
Anning, Mary 6–7
Benz, Bertha 28
chemistry 11
Clark, Eugenie 29
Clark, Mamie Phipps 14–15
computer 4, 8–9, 17
Curie, Marie 10–11, 26
Earle, Sylvia 22–23
elements 10
Goodall, Jane 20–21
invention 4, 8, 12–13, 28
Johnson, Katherine 16–17
Krafft, Katia 28
Lamarr, Hedy 12–13
Lovelace, Ada 8–9
math 4, 8, 14, 16–17, 29
physics 11, 26
school 5–6, 14–15, 18, 26
Tereshkova, Valentina 24–25
Tu, Youyou 18–19
West, Gladys 29
Wu, Sau Lan 26–27

READ MORE

Calvert, Jennifer. *Science Superstars: 30 Brilliant Women Who Changed the World.* New York: Castle Point Books, 2021.

Dickmann, Nancy. *Exploring Space: Women Who Led the Way (Super SHEroes of Science).* New York: Scholastic Inc., 2022.

Mann, Dionna L. *Hidden Heroes in Medicine (Who Else in History?).* Minneapolis: Lerner Publications, 2023.

LEARN MORE ONLINE

1. Go to **www.factsurfer.com** or scan the QR code below.
2. Enter "**Women in STEM**" into the search box.
3. Click on the cover of this book to see a list of websites.